LANDSCAPE DETECTIVE
Tracking Changes in your Surroundings

Alison Hawes

Crabtree Publishing Company
www.crabtreebooks.com

Author: Alison Hawes
Editor: Crystal Sikkens
Project coordinator: Kathy Middleton
Production coordinator: Ken Wright
Prepress technician: Margaret Amy Salter
Series consultant: Gill Matthews

Picture credits:
Corbis: Gideon Mendel 12
Istockphoto: 6l, Bart Coenders 5
Science Photo Library: Cordelia Molloy 16t
Shutterstock: (Cover), 6c, 6r, 7tc, 7tl, 7r,
  Natalia Bratslavsky 10t, juliengrondin 20, kavram 10br,
  Jacques Kloppers 15cl, Olga Lyubkina14, MaxFX 13br,
  Tan Wei Ming 4, Luciano Mortula 15cr,
  Edyta Pawlowska 7bg, Mark William Richardson 15b,
  Karen Roach 17c, Fred Sweet 21, Viktoriya 17b,
  Feng Yu 8c, Sergiy Zavgorodny 8t
Illustrations: Geoff Ward 9, Emma DeBanks 14t, 18–19

Library and Archives Canada Cataloguing in Publication

Hawes, Alison, 1952-
    Landscape detective : tracking changes in your surroundings / Alison Hawes.

(Crabtree connections)
Includes index.
ISBN 978-0-7787-9948-1 (bound).--ISBN 978-0-7787-9970-2 (pbk.)

    1. Geography--Juvenile literature. I. Title. II. Series: Crabtree connections

G133.H39 2010   j910   C2010-901513-4

Library of Congress Cataloging-in-Publication Data

Hawes, Alison, 1952-
 Landscape detective : tracking changes in your surroundings / Alison Hawes.
    p. cm. -- (Crabtree connections)
 Includes index.
 ISBN 978-0-7787-9970-2 (pbk. : alk. paper) -- ISBN 978-0-7787-9948-1 (reinforced library binding : alk. paper)
 1. Physical geography--Juvenile literature. I. Title. II. Series.

 GB58.H393 2011
 910'.02--dc22

                                                 2010008059

Crabtree Publishing Company

Printed in the U.S.A./062010/WO20100815

Published in Canada
Crabtree Publishing
616 Welland Ave.
St. Catharines, Ontario
L2M 5V6

Published in the United States
Crabtree Publishing
PMB 59051
350 Fifth Avenue, 59th Floor
New York, New York 10118

Contents

Landscape Detectives

Anyone can be a landscape detective.
All you need is

1. an interest in the world around you;

2. the right tools for the job.

Landscape detectives are interested in places and people. They are interested in weather, **habitats**, and the environment.

Sometimes landscape detectives **investigate** places and people close to where they live.

Sometimes they investigate people and places farther away.

These detectives are trying to find out what is happening in a **rain forest**.

To investigate the world around them, landscape detectives need to:

⇨ ask questions

⇨ gather evidence

⇨ look for clues

⇨ investigate why things happen

⇨ take measurements

A LANDSCAPE DETECTIVE'S TOOLS

- maps
- photographs
- digital camera
- video camera
- notebook
- clipboard
- compass
- computer
- measuring wheel
- rain gauge
- thermometer
- anemometer
- books
- DVDs and the Internet

Is your neighborhood changing?

Keep a photographic record of all new buildings, or old ones being pulled down. You can then look back at them to see how the neighborhood has changed.

230

Landscape detectives have many tools to help them investigate. Keep reading to find out how and when to use these tools.

220

Maps

Different maps give different kinds of information. Always read the title on a map, so that you choose the right map for the type of information you want.

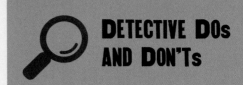
KNOW YOUR MAPS

Road maps

These maps show the streets in a city or town.

Atlases

These maps show the highways and interstates in a state or province.

Political maps

These maps use lines to separate places such as states and countries.

Scale

```
0 miles          50              100
|████████|░░░░░░░░|████████|
0 kilometers  50        100
```

Maps are drawn to different scales. You use a **scale** to find the distance between places on a map.

Choose a map with the right scale for the type of information you want.

Physical maps

These maps show landforms, such as mountains, and bodies of water.

Weather maps

These maps show what the weather is like in different areas.

Globes →

Use these to locate countries and oceans around the world.

A *small*-scale map shows a *large* area such as a country. A *large*-scale map shows a *small* area such as your neighborhood.

Using Maps

To help you use a map, you need to know about the points of a compass so you can follow directions.

You also need to know about grids, keys, and symbols so you can find places on a map more easily.

Compasses

A compass is a tool that helps you find and follow directions.

An eight-point compass →

NORTH

Northwest   Northeast

WEST   EAST

Southwest   Southeast

SOUTH

Compass points

The main points on a four-point compass are North, South, East, and West.

REMEMBER!
Most maps are drawn with North at the top.

8

Grids

Most maps have a grid of squares drawn on them. On some maps each square is given a number or a letter. On some maps each line of the grid is given two numbers.

DETECTIVE DOs AND DON'Ts

DO practice your map-reading skills with real maps. The next time you go on a trip, see if you can track your bus, car, or train route on a map.

FIND THE HOUSE

My house is on Rogate Road in square B5.

To find my house: Move your finger east, along the bottom of the map. Stop at square B. Now move your finger north to square 5.

Map Keys and Symbols

The key is the most important part of a map. It is the tool that tells you what all the symbols and colors on a map mean.

Always look at the key on a map. Maps hold a lot of information, but the key unlocks that information.

This map symbol shows you where a train station is.

This map symbol shows you where a wetland is.

TRY IT OUT!

Try the online map games at:

www.kidsgeo.com/geography-games/

Symbols

The symbols on a map can show you what a landscape looks like and what is in that area. Some symbols are simple pictures or shapes. Maps must show a lot of information, but there is not enough room on them for a lot of labels. So symbols are used instead.

KNOW YOUR SYMBOLS

Road

Highway

Some symbols give you information about roads.

Lighthouse

Windmill

Sch

School

Some symbols show you where important **landmarks** are.

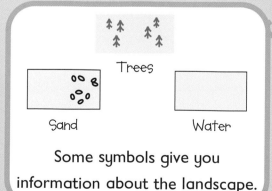

Trees

Sand

Water

Some symbols give you information about the landscape.

Theme park

Castle

Garden

Some symbols show you where places of interest are.

Photographs

Photographs are a good tool. They can help you learn more about the places and people around you. Landscape detectives use photographs taken from the ground and from the air.

Looking for clues

Photos taken at different times of the year might show you how places and people are affected by things like:

⇨ weather

⇨ pollution

⇨ tourism

This **aerial photograph** shows land affected by flooding.

Asking questions

A photograph can hold a lot
of information. To find out that
information, landscape detectives
ask questions about the
photographs they use.

⇨ Where were these photographs taken?

⇨ When were they taken?

⇨ What changes can you see in the photos?

⇨ Why have things changed?

⇨ Who has been affected by these changes?

⇨ How have they been affected?

Photographs taken from
space over time show that
the ice caps in the Arctic
are getting smaller.

TRY IT OUT!

Look for maps and
satellite photos of
where you live at:
http://maps.yahoo.com/

ice in the Arctic

REMEMBER!

Look for old photographs
of where you live at your
local museum.

Gathering Evidence

Landscape detectives have different ways of gathering **evidence**.

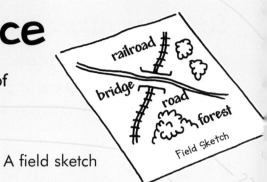

A field sketch

Field sketch

A field sketch is a drawing of the place you are investigating. Always label your sketch and give it a title.

You will need a:

⇨ clipboard

⇨ paper

⇨ pencil

⇨ eraser

⇨ a good pair of eyes!

This landscape detective is recording what he finds with his camera.

Survey

When doing a **survey**, make a table of the questions you are going to ask,

OR

of the things you want to find out.

DETECTIVE DOs AND DON'Ts

Before you use a digital camera:
DO check to see if there is room on the memory card;
DO make sure the battery is charged.

Cameras

Using a camera is an easy way of collecting evidence. Digital cameras are simple to use. They don't need film, and your pictures are stored on a memory card.

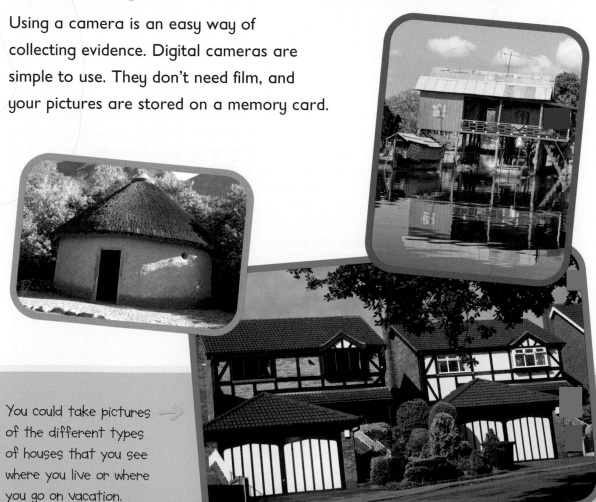

You could take pictures of the different types of houses that you see where you live or where you go on vacation.

Tools for Measuring

Landscape detectives also use tools for measuring things such as distance and the weather. Taking measurements is another way landscape detectives gather evidence.

Distance

Short lengths and depths can be measured with a ruler. Longer distances can be measured with a **measuring wheel**. A counter shows how far you have traveled when you push the wheel.

Rainfall

The tool for measuring rainfall is a **rain gauge**. It is a special plastic pot with a spike on the end. The spike is pushed into the ground to stop the gauge from blowing away. Rain falls into the gauge, and the amount is measured in millimeters, centimeters, or inches.

A counter on the measuring wheel tracks the distance it has traveled.

REMEMBER!

Don't put the rain gauge near buildings or trees that might protect it from the rain.

Temperature

The temperature of the air is measured with a **thermometer**.

TRY IT OUT!

Try some fun weather measuring activities at:

www.weatherwizkids.com/ weather-experiments.htm

Wind

You measure wind speed with an **anemometer**.

An anemometer measures wind speed in mph or KPH.

Displaying Information

Landscape detectives try to display the information they have collected to make it easy for everyone to understand. Some information is best displayed as a map or a plan. Other information is easier to understand if it is displayed as a diagram or graph.

Maps and plans

A map or plan is a good way of displaying information about a trip or a place.

My School

Railroad tracks

Steep hill going down

← This is a map of my route to school.

Playground

The Church

My House

The Town Hall

Graphs

A graph can be a good way to display the results of a survey. A graph makes it easier to understand the results. You can draw a graph on paper. Or you can draw a graph with the help of a computer program.

Diagrams

A diagram is a good way of displaying how something happens or how something works.

↓ This diagram shows what happens when we recycle paper.

These graphs show how a group of children travel to school. The same information is shown in three different ways.

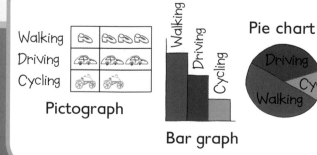

Walking		
Driving		
Cycling		

Pictograph

Walking
Driving
Cycling

Bar graph

Pie chart

Driving
Cycling
Walking

Searching for Information

Two of the best places for a landscape detective to find information are the library and the Internet.

Using the library

To find an information book in the library, look in the nonfiction section. All the books on these shelves are sorted by topic. This is so you can find what you are looking for more easily. Each nonfiction book also has a number on its spine. All the books on the same topic have the same number on the spine. A librarian can tell you which number to look for to find the information you want.

In the library you can find out about volcanoes by looking for books starting with the number 551.21.

Using the Internet

To find information on the Internet, type a question or some keywords into the search box. This will bring up a list of Web sites. Click on the Web site links to find the information you want.

DETECTIVE DOs AND DON'Ts

DO ask a librarian for help if you can't find the book you want.

The Internet gives you instant access to information from around the world.

Glossary

aerial photograph A photograph taken from the air

anemometer A tool for measuring the speed of the wind

evidence Information

habitat Where something lives

investigate To search and find out

landmark Something you can see that does not move

measuring wheel A tool for measuring long distances

rain forest A forest in a hot country that receives a lot of rain

rain gauge A tool for measuring how much rain has fallen

satellite photo A picture taken from space

scale The scale of a map shows how much the real size of a place has been shrunk to fit on a map

survey A list of questions given to a number of people

thermometer A tool for measuring temperature

Further Information

Web sites

You can look at a map of anywhere in the world, from your home town to a country many miles away at:
http://maps.google.com

Practice identifying continents, countries, states, and provinces at:
http://kids.nationalgeographic.com/Games/Geography Games/Geospy

Find out all about the weather at:
www.theweatherchannelkids.com

Books

All Over the Map series. Crabtree Publishing Company (2009)

Maps and Mapping by Deborah Chancellor. Kingfisher (2004)

Just the Facts: World Atlas by Dee Phillips. Ticktock (2006)

Follow the Map: Car Journey by Deborah Chancellor. Franklin Watts (2005)

220

Index

230